Creatin Children's Artwork Quilts

Shannon Gingrich Shirley

Foreword by Mary Kerr

Schiffer Publishing Ltd®

4880 Lower Valley Road • Atglen, PA 19310

Dedication

To my parents...
Who have always been there for me
with their enthusiastic support of my artistic
endeavors!

Frank and Jill Gingrich.
Photo courtesy of Rakhi Acharyya.

Acknowledgments

I would like to thank my daughters — Lauren, Emma, and Jenny — for their endless source of inspiration. Without your creative artistic skills, these quilts would not have been possible.

To all my friends and students who were so supportive and believed in me even when I was struggling, thank you... This would have been so much harder without you. I am forever grateful.

And lastly, to those of you who provided me with editorial advice, I cannot thank you enough for all of your help.

Published by Schiffer Publishing, Ltd.
4880 Lower Valley Road
Atglen, PA 19310
Phone: (610) 593-1777; Fax: (610) 593-2002
E-mail: Info@schifferbooks.com

Other Schiffer Books on Related Subjects:
A Quilted Memory: Ideas and Inspiration for Reusing Vintage Textiles, 978-0-7643-3921-9, $19.99
Vintage Children's Fabrics, 978-0-7643-3855-7, $29.99

Copyright © 2012 by Shannon Gingrich Shirley
Library of Congress Control Number: 2012945385

Designed by Mark David Bowyer
Type set in Tahoma BT / Zurich BT

ISBN: 978-0-7643-4180-9
Printed in China

For the largest selection of fine reference books on this and related subjects, please visit our website at:
www.schifferbooks.com.
You may also write for a free catalog.

This book may be purchased from the publisher.
Please try your bookstore first.

We are always looking for people to write books on new and related subjects.
If you have an idea for a book, please contact us at
proposals@schifferbooks.com.

Schiffer Books are available at special discounts for bulk purchases for sales promotions or premiums. Special editions, including personalized covers, corporate imprints, and excerpts can be created in large quantities for special needs. For more information contact the publisher.

In Europe, Schiffer books are distributed by
Bushwood Books
6 Marksbury Ave.
Kew Gardens
Surrey TW9 4JF England
Phone: 44 (0) 20 8392 8585; Fax: 44 (0) 20 8392 9876
E-mail: info@bushwoodbooks.co.uk
Website: www.bushwoodbooks.co.uk

Contents

Foreword

by Mary Kerr

Quilts, by their very nature, evoke a myriad of emotions. Shannon Shirley's children's artwork quilts reflect pure joy! I cannot help but smile when I look at the variety of textiles she has created to immortalize our children's creativity. She has found a way to capture the very essence of children's talents and the inherent pride in their artwork.

This book appeals to all of us. Every woman has, at one time, received a precious piece of children's artwork. These come from our children, nieces, nephews, or that special little one who lives down the block. They are presented to us as priceless works of art and we often lament the fact that these scraps of paper do not stand the test of time. Shannon has given us a way to allow these treasured pieces to graduate from the refrigerator to a place of honor on our walls.

Our home was always full of children's pictures that were taped to the walls and held with magnets to the refrigerator. At Christmastime, I brought out cherished holiday decorations the children had made and proudly hung them in our home …. a source of chagrin (and pride) when my teenagers saw their elementary school creations displayed each year. I asked Shannon to create three small quilts to showcase a favorite for each child. Today, those are the first decorations hung and are beautiful reminders of the small children who now bring their own babies to my home! The originals are crumbling, but the quilted creations will extend the memories for years to come.

I love what Shannon is teaching us to do! What better way to encourage the creativity of our children than honoring their inner artist with a quilt?

Introduction

I have always loved to create! Throughout my life I have been exposed to my parents' handiwork. My dad mainly worked with wood and was always busy making something. He used to say he could never work in fabric because it is too unpredictable. My mum always has some sort of needlework project going by hand or machine. I have been fortunate to learn many tips and techniques from them. I was introduced to quilting in 1985 when I helped my mum create a small quilt for my first child. My interest in quilting grew; however, with three small children, time and money were very limited. Keeping my projects small and simple, I taught myself new skills and techniques. Time and practice over the years has brought me to this point.

Having always loved the whimsical, quirky nature of young children's art, incorporating this artwork into my quilts became a passion. A child's enthusiasm is so contagious, and the artistic process is both inspiring and very energizing. I find working with children on these projects creates many special memories of time spent together and of the quilted item itself.

I have three daughters whose creative supply of inspiration is never-ending. When the girls were young, they often painted or drew directly on the fabric. Sometimes they would create a picture at school that they wanted to use in a quilt. I would trace the outline onto the fabric and they would recolor or repaint the image themselves. Occasionally they would lose interest and it would be left to me to finish. The girls loved giving gifts that they had helped to make and were very proud of their work.

As the years have passed and my daughters have grown, I continue to be inspired by their original pieces of art. I find myself going through stacks of pictures looking for a particular one I remember or simply searching for pieces to inspire an idea for a new children's artwork quilt.

These quilts are great fun to make and provide an opportunity to try a variety of techniques to recreate the original art. Always feel free to have fun, go bright, embellish, and enjoy! I am happy to share the different techniques and materials I use, plus offer you a variety of layouts so you'll have plenty of ideas for your next quilt.

Most pieces of children's art are not made with archival quality supplies so they deteriorate over time. Colors fade and paper becomes very fragile. You cannot preserve every piece of art made, nor would you want to, but sometimes a particular piece just reaches out and speaks to your heart. Maybe it makes you laugh or perhaps it records a particular event. You just know it when you see it and you feel an instant connection. There are many reasons why you might choose a piece of art to recreate. Are you redecorating a bathroom? Maybe beach themed artwork will inspire you. Making pieces to use as gifts may highlight other pictures the children in your life have created. My youngest daughter and I wanted to make a collection of seasonal quilts so we collected pictures representing various times of the year. When we couldn't find one for a particular season, she was more than willing to draw one right on the fabric using fabric markers or fabric paint Whatever your reasons, you will find these quilts fun to make. They will bring you, the children involved, and others many years of memories and smiles.

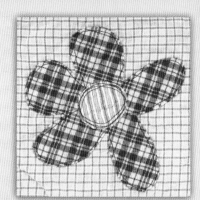

Chapter 1

Artwork Selection and Technique

There are dozens, if not hundreds, of great how-to-quilt books on the market. My intent is that you will use your favorite one in combination with this book to inspire you to incorporate children's artwork into your quilts and other fiber art projects. There is such freedom to children's artwork and endless ways to interpret all of the color and fun into projects that will honor the children who created the original pieces of art.

When I began incorporating children's artwork into my quilts, I had limited techniques in my repertoire. I wanted to reproduce the art as close to the original piece as possible. Using the same method as the original makes it easy to do this. For your first project, consider choosing a piece of art that was drawn with markers since it is the easiest method to begin with. Permanent fabric markers dry fast, stay soft and pliable, and are washable. Using crayons or colored pencils is also quick and easy; however, they should only be used for art quilts you intend to hang on the wall as the colors fade noticeably if washed regularly. If absolutely necessary, art quilts made with crayons or pencils can be gently hand washed so they don't lose too much of their color.

While it is your artistic choice to use the method you like to create your quilt, consider the amount of time you have to complete the project, its intended purpose, who the recipient is, and what supplies you have on hand. You may need to finish a small gift for grandma in the next two days because your daughter just drew a precious picture of the two of them planting flowers together. Choosing to recreate the picture with needle turn appliqué or hand embroidery is probably not practical if you have a busy life; but taking out your fabric markers and tracing the picture onto muslin and adding a colorful floral border in grandma's favorite colors will work wonderfully. If it is a very small piece, hand quilting might be an option, but machine quilting is faster and can add fun details to the piece. Traditional binding might be the look you are going for, but perhaps a quicker method would make it possible to finish on time. Imagine how excited your daughter will be to give her grandma a gift she helped to create!

Over the years, I have learned many techniques and edge finishes and experimented with those that suit the particular project I was working on at the time. The options are endless. I use hand and machine quilting, traditional and fusible appliqué, hand embroidery, machine couching, crayons, markers, colored pencils, paints, and embellishments to recreate the pictures I find so inspiring.

Basic Drawing

A Little Birdie #1, 14" x 17". **Original artwork by Emma Shirley, age 7.** The original piece of art was drawn using markers so reproducing it in permanent fabric markers was a natural first choice. The picture was traced directly onto the white fabric with markers and then a simple border was added. The edge was finished using an escape hatch method. Rick rack was added to mimic an accent border. The piece was finished with minimal machine quilting to include edge stitching to resemble binding and to keep the edges from turning. This was a quick and simple project.

Fusible Appliqué with Free Motion Machine Stitching

A Little Birdie #2, 9" x 12". For this technique I chose to use Heat n Bond®, a lightweight paper backed fusible product, and fabrics that would remind me of actual textures of the objects in the picture. The entire picture was fused in place and layered with batting and backing. I then added texture and details with free motion stitching. The edge was finished with a straight line of stitching using a walking foot and then trimmed with a pinking rotary cutter. The final step was to use Fray Block® on the raw edge.

A Little Birdie #2, pinking rotary cutter, Fray Block®.

Detail of edge.

Thread Sketching

A Little Birdie #3, 9" x 12". Tracing the picture onto the fabric with a blue water soluble marker is a very simple method of preparation. After tracing, this picture was then layered with batting and backing. I then used free motion thread sketching in black and white thread to create the picture and the background texture. I chose to bind it with a traditional bias binding because I love the way striped fabrics wind around the edge of the quilt when used this way.

Fusible Appliqué with Hand Embroidery

A Little Birdie #4, 14" x 17". This quilt was made using lightweight fusible appliqué like the earlier piece, but instead of free motion machine stitching, I chose to hand embroider it using blanket and outline stitches. Typically I use two strands of embroidery floss, but for smaller details like the baby bird and eggs, I used one strand. After finishing the embroidery, I added a scalloped border using vintage feed sack fabric, which I thought suited the reproduction fabrics used to create the picture. The vintage feel of this quilt and its small size helped me decide to hand quilt it. The edge was finished with a scalloped facing leaving a nice clean knife edge.

Hand Embroidered

Fabric Painting
– Enlarged Image

A Little Birdie #6, **nightshirt.** For this nightshirt project, I enlarged a tracing of the original picture by 200% on a printer in my home and taped the pages together. I then slid these papers inside the nightshirt making it possible to see the picture to paint from and also keep the paint from seeping through to the back of the nightshirt.

A Little Birdie #5, 12" x 15". The final quilt in this group was traced onto white fabric using a #2 pencil. It could have also been traced using permanent colored Micron pens; saving you from checking back to the original to see what color embroidery floss to use. The entire picture was hand embroidered using the outline stitch. A scrappy chevron border was added before the quilt was layered and minimally free motion quilted using clear monofilament thread. Black rick rack was top stitched in place and a mitered corner facing finished the edge. The choices are endless; enjoy using them!

This is a great project to do with kids. When my three daughters were young, they loved to get involved with special projects and gifts. Their favorite technique was using fabric paint and often their project of choice was painting nightshirts for themselves or for Grandma and me. We used the type of paint that you squirted directly out of the bottle onto the fabric. However, we chose to squirt out small amounts on plastic lids and use fabric brushes to apply a lighter coat of paint. These days I use Tulip's® So Soft paint, which is a much softer paint and permanent when dry. It is readily available in local craft stores.

Fusible Appliqué with Machine Zigzag Stitch

A Little Birdie #7, apron. I incorporated this same picture into an apron. It was made using a lightweight fusible product and fabrics that do not resemble the textures of the original picture. I used a small machine zigzag stitch to sew down the fusible appliqué pieces. Details, like the legs and small branches, were drawn with permanent fabric markers, and then I added a zigzag stitch over the marker for a cohesive look.

Fusible Appliqué – Reduced Image

Front and back views of *A Little Birdie #8* postcard, 4" x 6". Reducing the size of original pictures is always an option. Fabric postcards to send through the mail are a great small project. This particular postcard was made by reducing the original by 50% and using fusible appliqué and free motion stitching. Peltex 72®, a two-sided heavy weight fusible interfacing was used as the center layer in this project.

Original artwork by Emma Shirley
recreated by Shannon Shirley 2014

POSTCARDS
by SHANNON

Basic Drawing – Reduced Image

When you reduce a drawing significantly, it helps to simplify the drawing before reducing it.

   There are endless ways to incorporate children's artwork into your fiber art projects. I hope to inspire you to try new techniques or go back to a technique you haven't used in a while. I am a quilter, so naturally most of my projects have been quilts, but I am always ready to try something new! Be open to learning from anyone and from anywhere. You'll be amazed at the techniques and tips you can find and learn over time. Have fun with these projects, be adventurous, relax, and enjoy...be a kid! Honoring the children in your life and the lives of others by incorporating their artwork into your projects will bring happiness and treasured memories for everyone involved.

A Little Birdie #9, **name tag**. Name tags and bookmarks are also fun and easy. They are a great use for fusible scraps from other projects. For this name tag, the original picture was reduced 75% and traced onto white fabric with fabric markers. Scraps of fusible fabrics made up the remainder of the design. A small machine zigzag stitch was used to sew down the raw edges and also to finish the edge.

Chapter 2

Preparation, Tools, and Tips

Original art and plastic sheet protector. No matter what method you choose for recreating artwork, you need to begin by protecting the original art. If the original fits into a plastic page protector, that's a great option, but if it will not, here are some options to consider.

Original art and a color copy. If the original consists of colors on white paper, a copy made on a printer works great. You just need to be aware that the colors sometimes don't copy true, so you may need to refer back to the original to choose the colors for your project.

Original art with tracing paper and clear plastic for tracing. Pencil drawings or other art pieces without much contrast between the background color and the drawing should be carefully traced onto tracing paper. Use a pencil, not a marker, to make sure nothing bleeds through onto the original piece of art. If you cannot see the image through tracing paper you can use clear plastic and carefully use a permanent marker.

Redraw pencil lines in permanent marker. If you used tracing paper and pencil to copy the image, you will want to retrace the pencil lines using a permanent marker at this time. Doing so will make it easier to get clear enlargements or see the picture through light colored material. Before you start to redraw the lines with marker, put the original artwork out of the way to protect it.

Multiple enlarged copies taped together. If I am keeping the piece of artwork its original size and it will fit on my printer, I make a copy to work from. If the original piece is too large for a single copy, I make copies of each section of the original and tape them together. You can also enlarge the original drawing as big as you choose and tape the pieces together. Occasionally a piece is three-dimensional and therefore can't fit into a printer so take a photograph of the piece and work from the enlarged photograph.

Whether to enlarge, reduce, or maintain the original size of the artwork depends upon a number of factors you may want to consider. What are you going to do with the project? Will this piece be part of a set of quilts that need to be finished to a specific size? Will this be a collection of blocks used to create a traditional quilt? Is the quilt part of a challenge with specific rules that must be adhered to? Another consideration might be, does the piece have hand or footprints from a child? If so, it is nice to keep the prints in their original size as it captures a specific time in the child's life.

When enlarging or reducing a piece of artwork, I use a variety of tools:

- TRACER PROJECTOR for enlarging.
  These are available at local craft stores.

- OVERHEAD PROJECTOR for enlarging. Check at yard sales or online sites like Craigslist.

- COPIER with enlarging/reducing capability; tape sections together if necessary.

- ARTIST PROPORTIONAL SCALE. This makes it easy to calculate what percentage to enlarge or reduce the original artwork by.

If you don't have any of these items available, go to a local printer shop; they will enlarge or reduce the artwork for you.

Tracer Projector and Enlarger®.

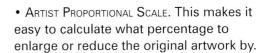 

Quilter's Assistant Proportional Scale®.

Tips for Projects with Applied Color

When working with fabric marker, fabric paint, pencil or crayon, here are some helpful hints.

Fabric grain. Be sure to create the picture on the fabric squares keeping the straight grain going from the top to the bottom of each square and the cross grain going from side to side. This will make constructing the quilt easier.

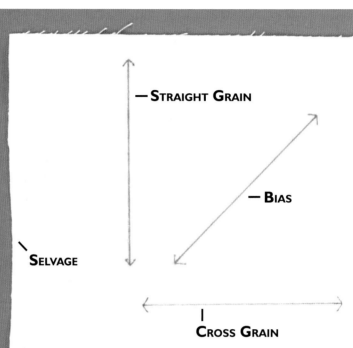

— **STRAIGHT GRAIN**

— **BIAS**

SELVAGE

CROSS GRAIN

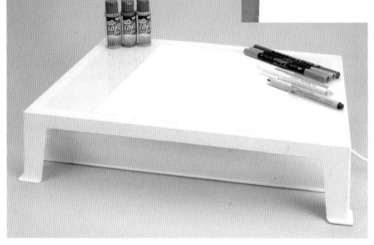

Transfer the picture to light fabric using a light box. To transfer a picture to a light colored fabric, use a light box, a window or a glass top table. Sometimes, I use a blue water soluble marker but I have also been known to paint or draw right on the fabric without tracing it first.

Transfer the picture to dark material using Saral® wax free transfer paper. Transferring a picture to dark material can be achieved by using a product called Saral® wax free transfer paper. Place the paper, color side down, between a copy of the original picture and the front of the fabric and trace over the picture with a pencil or a stylus.

If you oversize your pieces of fabric, draw the finished size square lightly on the fabric. I find that cutting the squares oversized is not necessary. Because the squares of fabric are not handled a lot, I don't need to re-trim the fraying. If you do choose to oversize them, make sure to gently mark the actual size of the finished square on the fabric. Children tend to draw all the way to the edge of the fabric allowing important details or letters to be lost as they are sewn into the seam allowances.

Iron freezer paper on the back of the fabric squares. Freezer paper can be ironed on to the back of the squares to stabilize the fabric so that drawing and painting is easier.

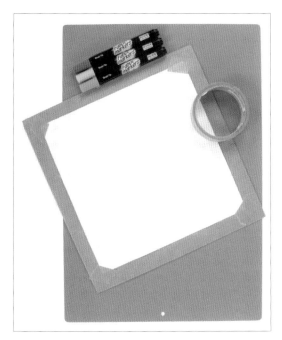

Tape fabric squares to cardboard. Taping the fabric down to a piece of cardboard can also keep it from moving around, which helps when kids are drawing or painting. Plus the cardboard can be turned easily to access different areas of the picture, and it protects the surface under your painting.

Selection of fabric markers I use. For many years I have used Fabric Mate® Markers or Marvy® Markers in my projects. They are available at local craft stores. They are easy to use, stay soft, and are permanent when dry. All markers can dry out over time when not being used, so always be sure to cap them tightly. Recently I purchased Fabrico® Markers at a national quilt show. I've been told that if they are stored horizontally that they will last longer than the other brands. They also have a different sized tip on each end, which is useful. Micron® pens are my favorite for fine lines and details.

Selection of colored pencils I use. Over the years I have taken many technique classes. Often the instructor would have us add small details with colored pencils. Crayola® pencils work fine, but Prismacolor® pencils go on the fabric more easily and have more pigment in them. Even though these are not permanent, it's a good idea to heat set them by covering the drawing with paper towels and using a dry iron. Recently I purchased Inktense® water soluble ink pencils. With these pencils you first draw with them, then add water to get a watercolor look, and finally you heat set them and they are permanent.

Selection of crayons I use. When it comes to crayons, much like most pencils, you must remember that they are not permanent but you still need to heat set them by covering them with a paper towel and pressing them with a hot dry iron. Crayola® crayons work fine however Prang® crayons have more pigment in them, go on a little easier and produce a slightly more vibrant color.

Selection of fabric paints I use. When I started painting on fabric, it was with my children, so I purchased fabric paints at local craft shops. They used to dry very stiff especially if the paint was applied too thickly. These days I use Tulip® So Soft paints, because they are readily available, dry soft, and are permanent when dry. I have also experimented with Jacquard® paints and Seta Color® paints, with good results. *Note: Too much paint can leave the fabric stiff, so some supervision of the children when they are painting is helpful if you want the fabric to maintain a soft hand. If letting kids loose on fabric with permanent paint is just too stressful for you, then having the kids draw or paint on paper and recreating them on fabric yourself might be a more relaxing option for you as it gives you more control over the finished project.*

Tips for Projects with Fusible Appliqué

Collect possible supplies for inspiration. When I'm starting a fusible appliqué project, I like to collect any materials I think I might like to use. While I am preparing the fusible pieces, I often get inspiration from the fabrics and notions along with the original art.

Reverse original image before tracing if using a fusible product. When using fusible appliqué, remember to reverse your original picture before tracing it onto the lightweight fusible product. This ensures that your picture will be the correct direction when finished.

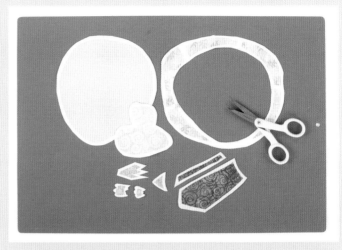

Cut out all of your appliqué pieces on the pencil lines. Now it is very easy to see that the adhesive is just around the edge of each appliqué piece. Peel off the remaining paper and get ready to put your picture together. Be sure to save the scraps as they are great for small projects like postcards.

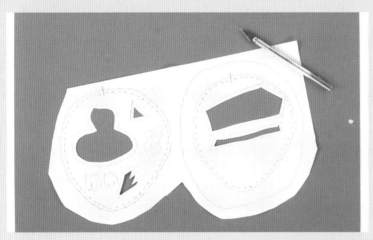

Cut away centers of fusible product using a small detail knife. After tracing the reverse images onto the fusible paper, consider cutting away the center of the fusible to maintain the softness in the appliqué pieces. For wall quilts some artists like the additional stiffness of the fusible layers. I prefer to cut away the centers especially when layering multiple pieces. I find that using a small detail knife is easier than using small detail scissors. Leave about 1/4" inside the traced lines of larger pieces and don't bother to trim away the centers of smaller pieces. If you are not going to cut away the centers, then you cannot trace smaller pieces inside of larger ones like you see in the picture. Trace each piece separately.

Press fusible product to back side of your chosen fabrics. As you do so, leaving a little extra fusible around the edges makes this process easier. Remember to follow the instructions for the brand of fusible you are using as they are brand specific.

If you can see your drawing through the fabric, you can use this to layout the appliqué pieces.

Use a non-stick pressing sheet to join the appliqué pieces together and then move them as a whole unit.

If you cannot see through the fabric, place the drawing onto of the fabric and lift it carefully to layout your appliqué pieces.

Audition whole appliqué unit on possible background fabrics.

After drawing some of the smaller details on with a fabric marker, I then zigzag stitched over it. Depending on the size of the pieces, it may be necessary to add some of the details using permanent fabric markers. You can decide later whether to stitch over the marker or not. On this piece, I drew the feathers on the birds' heads, legs, and the black in the eyes with marker and then stitched over them.

Tips for Projects with Embroidery

When hand embroidering, I mainly use the outline stitch and french knots. Hand blanket stitch is what I prefer when finishing raw edge appliqué pieces. I like to use two strands of embroidery floss on most projects. Occasionally I use one strand for fine details like whiskers or three to six strands if I want a very bold look. Whether you use an embroidery hoop is up to you. I prefer to keep my project loose. Hand embroidery is easily transportable and can be taken along wherever you are going. Like any new skill, it will become easier the more familiar you become with it, so just keep practicing.

Label on *A Little Bird #4*. Adding labels to your quilts is always a good idea. Include a minimum of who made it and when it was made. Labels can be very detailed, telling the story behind the quilt or decorating them to coordinate with the quilt. It is just one more place you can get creative and have some fun. Throughout the book are examples of various labels.

Outline stitch. Detail of *A Little Birdie #5*.

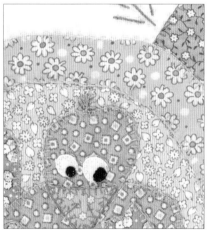

Blanket stitch. Detail of *A Little Birdie #4*.

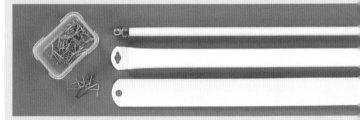

Selection of products I use to hang my small art quilts. When I make art quilts, I like to put a narrow sleeve on the back of the quilt to enable me to hang them up and enjoy them. Because many of my pieces are seasonal and I like to move them around to new locations, I use 1/2" sequin pins to hang the quilts up with. By doing this there are only very small holes left in the wall. I use these pins to hold quilts up to about four feet wide. I use a variety of different rods to hang my small quilts on. Round sash rods are readily available anywhere curtain rods are sold. Flat sash rods by Kirsch® are harder to find but can be ordered. They come in two sizes and are very sturdy.

As you can see there are quite a number of techniques, products, and tools to choose from. Don't be overwhelmed with all of the options; just choose a starting place and go from there. Over time try techniques you are not familiar with. These projects are a great place to practice your skills or try new products. Remember, relax and have fun!

Preparing the vinyl slat to use as a quilt rod. My choice for my small art quilts up to 14" wide is to use old vinyl mini blinds cut to fit each quilt. Measure the width of the quilt and cut the vinyl slat a 1/2" shorter than that measurement. Trim the ends to a smooth semi circle using any paper scissors. Use a hole punch to put a hole in each end of the vinyl slat to enable you to hang it on the pins. Occasionally, I use two slats taped together to support the weight of a quilt and keep it from sagging.

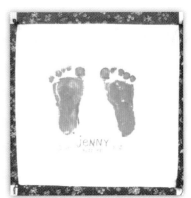

Chapter 3
Keeping it Simple

Being self-taught, my early projects were simple, but I still love them nonetheless. The first quilt project using children's artwork that I remember making was for my dad in 1992. It was a few months before Christmas. Trying to think of what to get for someone who has everything he needs was challenging me. My mom suggested making him a quilt to cuddle with when he was napping. There were only two quilts I had made up to this point. Both were squares of fabric pieced into a quilt top, layered with batting and backing, and tied with cotton yarn; so that's what I decided to do. I calculated the size of the quilt based on finished 10" squares and decided that eight rows of five squares each would be a good size. Alternating a multicolored print fabric with muslin squares featuring my girls' original artwork meant we needed to have twenty picture blocks.

Involving all three of my girls in this secret plan, we began working on the squares for our quilt. Using a black Micron® pen and fabric paints, my oldest daughter Lauren, who was six at the time, made eight squares for the quilt. My middle daughter, Emma, who was four, made eight squares as well. I helped my youngest daughter, Jenny, who had just turned one, create three squares to put in Grandpa's quilt. The last block was used as the label with all of the information about the quilt. Grandpa loved his quilt and used it daily for eighteen years. The pictures have faded and, sadly, my dad died in 2010, but the quilt will always bring us happy memories.

Grandpa's Quilt, 50" x 80", 1992.

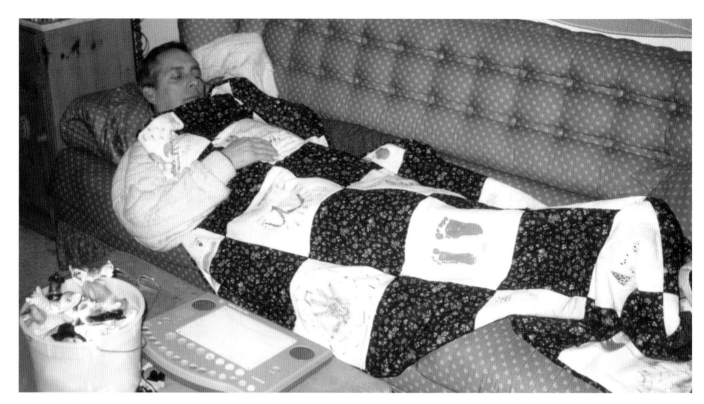

Grandpa testing his new quilt.

This quilt was made with
lots of love for
Grandpa Frank Gingrich

The idea was from
Grandma Jill Gingrich
The time was made possible by
Mitch Shirley
The sewing and guidance was by
Shannon Shirley
And the artwork was designed
and painted by
Lauren, Emma and Jenny Shirley

Merry Christmas 1992
We love you!

Label on *Grandpa's Quilt*.

Details of *Grandpa's Quilt*, original art by Lauren Shirley, age 6.

Details of *Grandpa's Quilt*, original art by Emma Shirley, age 4.

Details of *Grandpa's Quilt*, original art by Jenny Shirley, age 1.

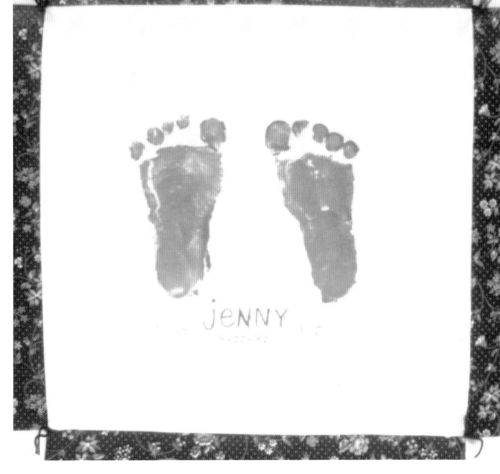

Most of my early projects were small and portable, so I could practice my skills anywhere and everywhere my children needed to be during their busy childhoods.

This group of seasonal quilts was made with the artistic help of my youngest daughter Jenny.

Fall, 17" x 17", 1997. Original art by Jenny Shirley, age 6. Jenny was inspired! She decided to draw a fall quilt on paper, complete with a border that had a leaf in each corner. I transferred the picture to the muslin using a fine tip permanent marker. Using squeeze bottle fabric paints, we decided it would be better for Jenny to paint the picture with a paintbrush. I added a light brushing of blue for the sky and a bit of green grass. A combination of hand and machine quilting was used on this piece. It was also embellished with scraps of fabric to represent leaves, and of course we appliquéd a leaf in each corner, just like her original picture.

Back to School, 17" x 17", 1997. Original art by Jenny Shirley, age 5. The first quilt was made when Jenny's two older sisters started back to school one September. Jenny wanted to ride on a school bus, but she had another year to wait before she would be old enough. She drew a picture of herself and her friends on the bus. She didn't like the faces she drew, so we selected faces from the novelty print we had chosen for the border fabric. We worked together to reproduce the bus in fabric. Jenny colored some of the background using permanent fabric markers. The words were written on a separate piece of paper that I then traced onto the fabric. Minimal hand quilting was done on this piece. Jenny completed the picture by adding a rainbow and the ladybugs. You could tell it is going to be a wonderful day riding the school bus!

Happy Easter, 17" x 17", 1998. Original art by Jenny Shirley, age 6. *Happy Easter* was originally a pencil drawing. I transferred the picture to the fabric using a fine tip marker, and Jenny painted the picture herself. I added the words that she wrote on a piece of scrap paper.

Happy Thanksgiving, 17" x 17", 1999. Original artwork by Jenny Shirley, age 8. *Happy Thanksgiving* was an adaptation of the cover from a school project. I loved the picture and wanted a quilt to hang in November, so I transferred the picture to the fabric. Since I had not yet learned that I could use crayon on fabric, I chose to color it using permanent fabric markers because of how quick and easy they were to work with.

Happy Valentines, 17" x 17", 2000. **Original artwork by Jenny Shirley, age 8.** Jenny gave me this picture of the two of us together, and it inspired another seasonal quilt. After enlarging this pencil drawing, I was preparing to transfer and color it myself, but Jenny decided she wanted to color the picture herself. She also decided that she no longer liked the original sun so she drew a different one. When I told Jenny this quilt would hang in February, she decided to add a groundhog as well.

Happy 4th of July, 17" x 17", 2000. **Original art by Jenny Shirley, age 8.** Jenny drew this particular picture right on the fabric using fabric markers. She wanted to add some color to the sky and the street, but she didn't know how. I showed her a dry brush stippling technique using fabric paint. As Jenny was finishing the details with the fabric markers, the colors ran onto the face of the little girl. Jenny was ready to throw the whole project away, but I helped her remake the face and fuse it over the original smeared face. She was happy and so was I. After hand quilting this piece, beaded embellishments were added to the fireworks.

Let it Snow, 17" x 17", 2004. Original art by Jenny Shirley, age 11. The last quilt in the series was a snowman Jenny drew. I recreated it using fusible fabric appliqué. It has a three-dimensional hat and scarf, hand embroidery, couched yarns, and gold snowflake embellishments. Most of it is hand quilted, but I also added a bit of free motion quilting on the snowman and his mittens.

April Showers, **17" x 17", 2003. Original artwork by Jenny Shirley, age 10.** Earlier I mentioned that sometimes a piece of children's original work will speak to your heart and you just know that this is one that you would like to recreate to preserve it and honor it. The letter, that Jenny left for me the day she headed back to school after winter break, was one of those pieces. How sweet that she would think about leaving me a note to brighten my day! We decided that we could add a little rain off to the side and a couple more flowers, and this could become our spring quilt. Every time I get this quilt out, I am reminded of that letter that made me smile and touched my heart. Jenny had lost interest in recreating pictures by this age so I did this one on my own. Hand quilting and beading were used again, but I added a narrow purple flange which was a new technique I had learned.

Chapter 4

Adding New Techniques

In 2004, I decided it was time to start taking classes. Whenever I could find the time and money, I signed up for classes, which added new techniques and a surge of new inspiration for my quilting. I never really saw myself as someone who would make art quilts, but I was intrigued by the quilts I was seeing at some of the large quilt shows and wanted to understand how they were made. After just two classes, I was hooked! Sometimes I signed up for classes even if I didn't like the project just to learn different techniques because I knew that someday I might use the information from that class to create another original quilt.

Original artwork by Jenny Shirley, age 6. One summer afternoon, I was cleaning out a closet and came across this picture Jenny had drawn in kindergarten. It brought back such fond memories and put a smile on my face.

Christmas in Kindergarten, 19" x 14", 2004. I was still thinking about it the next day, so I went to my stash of fabric to see if anything caught my eye as possible fabrics to make an artwork quilt. I found a piece that was bluish gray with white flecks on it, which would work perfectly for the background, but when I found the bright green with colorful dots already on it for the tree, I got so inspired I had to start working on it right away. Two days later it was done. I used fusible appliqué and free motion top stitching to hold the pieces in place. Free motion quilting created texture in the background. To finish this piece, I added white fabric paint because it just wasn't "snowy" enough, and then bound it with the background fabric. This particular art quilt is one of my favorites and continues to make me smile as I relive fond memories.

Living is Love, 16" x 12", 2006. This piece of art was drawn by my niece, Rebecca, when she was seven, as part of a poetry book she made to give my daughter Jenny for her fourteenth birthday. Rebecca's mom loved this particular picture and poem so for her next birthday I made this art quilt to surprise her. The hat and bow are made with fusible appliqué fabric and the inside of the hat was lightly colored with a fabric marker. Words were traced onto the fabric using a permanent fabric marker and then free motion stitched to give them dimension. The background and border are free motion quilted with a small floral design inspired by the border fabric.

**Original artwork by
Rebecca Shirley, age 7, 2005.**

Label on *Living is Love*.

Let it Glow, 26" x 28", 2006. **Original artwork by Emma Shirley, age 5, 1994.** My daughters loved to get involved in gift-giving especially when it involved artwork. They would paint nightshirts for my mum and me to sleep in. This was painted by my daughter Emma for Grandma when she was about five. Years later it was retired to a drawer. Mum could not part with it because she and my dad had always gotten a giggle whenever she wore it to bed. Why you ask? When they would turn off the lights, grandma would be covered in glowing spots because the snow was painted with glow in the dark paint! I repurposed the nightshirt into a wall hanging by adding a border and using free motion quilting to add texture. The final touch was a fringe of white pompoms reminiscent of snow balls.

Every year my friend Mary Kerr hangs up a collection of elementary artwork that her three children made years ago. Some of the pieces are starting to deteriorate, but hanging the artwork is a tradition in their home. Mary asked me to create three art quilts. She gave me three pieces of artwork and a couple of yards of vintage Santa fabric that belonged to the children's great grandmother to incorporate into the quilts. I decided that because the angel and the reindeer had tracings of hand and footprints, they needed to remain their original size; after all, this recorded a specific time in her children's lives. This decision meant that the Santa would need to be reduced to fit the same size background in order for all three quilts to be the same size. Each quilt also has the child's name on it in their own handwriting. If the piece you are reproducing isn't signed, try to find a signature on other artwork the child created at the same age.

On all three quilts, I used fusible appliqué with machine blanket stitch along the raw edges. The details like Katherine's and Ryan's signatures and the reindeer's mouth were done with free motion zigzag over fabric marker to resemble satin stitch. The angel's hair is couched embroidery floss and her face is drawn with crayons. The reindeer's bow tie and Sean's name were drawn with fabric markers. Santa's beard, mustache, and pompom are made three dimensional by fusing two pieces of white fabric together and leaving the edges raw. After twisting and turning the beard strips, they are tacked in place to keep them from falling back straight. Twelve Santa's are fussy cut from the vintage fabric and blanket stitched in the corners of each of the quilts. I hope these art quilts will bring many years of happy memories and that their family tradition will carry on with a new twist.

Original artwork by Ryan Kerr, age 8, 1997. *Ryan's Santa,* 16" x 22", 2008.

Original artwork by Katherine Kerr, age 5, 1991. *Katherine's Angel*, **16" x 22", 2008.**

Original artwork by Sean Kerr, age 7, 1994. *Sean's Reindeer*, **16" x 22", 2008.**

These next three quilts were made when I began lecturing about children's artwork quilts and needed more samples. My youngest daughter Jenny had started a collection of quilt squares when she was four years old because she was going to make her own quilt like grandpa's. She was eighteen when I turned these squares into a collection of wall hangings and she still enjoys them as do I.

Jinx, 17" x 17", 2009. Original artwork by Jenny Shirley, age 4, 1995. Jinx was our next door neighbor's cat. Jenny drew the original picture when she was four, but it never was transferred to fabric, so I recreated this one on my own. Instead of drawing the squiggles in the background, I decided to embellish the quilt with couched embroidery floss to resemble the picture. I left the tail of the floss hanging loose because cats love dangling strings.

Oatmeal, 17" x 17", 2009. Original artwork by Jenny Shirley, age 4, 1995. Oatmeal was our pet rabbit. When Jenny was four she drew the original picture. I transferred the outline onto the quilt square and Jenny painted it herself.

Maggie, 17" x 17", 2009. Original artwork by Jenny Shirley, age 7, 1999. Maggie was Grandma's and Grandpa's golden retriever. Jenny painted directly onto the fabric when she was seven. She used a Micron® pen for the fine details and fabric markers for Maggie's name.

SNOW, 13" x 17", 2010. **Original artwork by Lauren Shirley, 1996.** While in elementary school my oldest daughter wrote quite a few acrostic poems. They were not her favorite, but I saved some of them nonetheless. "SNOW" was recreated by tracing the original words on one piece of tracing paper, reducing it slightly, and then tracing the blue snow onto another piece. I traced the picture and words onto the fabric using permanent fabric markers. After adding an appropriate "snowy" border, I chose to embroider some of the snow and add the silver shadow on the S, N, O, and W. I then layered the quilt top with batting and backing. Hand quilting was done using embroidery floss in two shades of blue and white, and snowflake brads from the scrapbooking section of the local craft store were added embellishments.

Halloween, 13" x 16", 2011. **Original artwork by Lauren Shirley, 1995.** *Halloween* was traced onto a light green material with permanent fabric markers and bordered with a green print. The escape hatch method quickly finished the edges. I free motion quilted it with 50-weight cotton thread and then embellished the quilt with purple rick rack to resemble an accent border. I also embroidered black lines for the spider buttons to hang from.

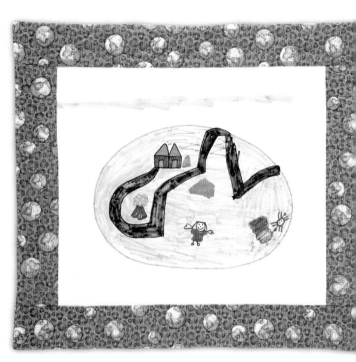

Lauren's World, **18" x 16", 2011. Original artwork by Lauren Shirley, age 4, 1991.** Lauren had a very clear vision of the world at age four. It was round and the sky and sun were above it. Her house was on the earth and there was a long road past a tree and a lake to get to the beach where there was a crab. Lauren has always loved the beach and water and still does as an adult. I chose to recreate this piece in fabric markers to resemble the original as closely as possible. It is bordered with an Earth friendly recycling novelty print because being green is important to her.

Leaning Flowers, **24" x 17", 2011. Original artwork by Emma Shirley, age 3, 1991.** Emma drew this picture using markers when she was three years old. That same year I painted it onto a nightshirt for Emma to give to her Grandma for Christmas. Emma was 24 when I repurposed the nightshirt into a wall-hanging for my mum. The T-shirt was stabilized using a lightweight fusible stabilizer before it was trimmed to size. I added an accent border of orange, picked up from the border fabric. The piece is free motion quilted with cotton threads to blend with the background colors.

***Two by Two*, 18" x 30", 2010. Original artwork by Lauren Shirley, age 5, 1991.** Another formal challenge inspired me to use a piece of children's artwork that I had tucked away years ago. The theme of the challenge was "Two by Two" and the quilts had to be 18" x 30" with a vertical orientation. My first thought was Noah's Ark, and it just so happened that my nursery was decorated in that theme for our third child. My oldest daughter was very excited about the baby and drew this picture to hang in the nursery. I had always intended to recreate this piece of artwork but had never gotten around to it so this was the extra push I needed to get it done. I wanted to use the whole ark and spent weeks doodling ideas for various possibilities but none of them pleased me. Instead I decided to do an adaptation of the picture for my quilt. Techniques used in this quilt were fusible appliqué with hand blanket stitch, hand embroidery, machine free motion quilting and a facing to finish the edge.

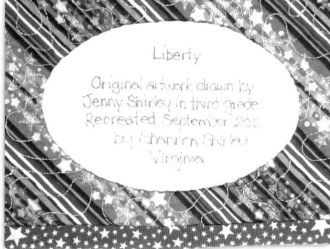

Liberty, 11" x 24", 2011. **Original artwork by Jenny Shirley, age 9, 2001.** We went on a trip with Jenny for spring break when she was in third grade. During the trip she kept a journal with pictures and notes about our adventures. One of the pictures she drew was the Statue of Liberty with Jenny herself, peeking out of the window in the crown. I enlarged the original drawing by 200% and traced it onto the fabric with a navy blue Micron® pen and then colored it with Fabrico® permanent fabric markers. I enlarged the word Liberty by 850% and left the sentence about the window its original size. The hand embroidery was done with 1-2 strands of navy blue floss.

Chapter 5

Combining Multiple Pieces of Art

After making my first children's artwork quilt in 1992, I had not combined multiple pieces of artwork into one quilt until now, nineteen years later.

I Love You Dad, 17" x 20", 2008. Original artwork by **Logan Delery, age 8.** Logan is an amazing athlete in a number of sports. He and his dad love to throw a football together and in one of the drawings Gilbert, their dog, is joining in the fun. I used fabric markers to recreate these pictures and sashed them with a navy blue print. A novelty football print border was the perfect choice. This quilt has a combination of hand and machine quilting.

My Daddy, 18" x 18", 2008. This piece was finished with minimal hand quilting and a striped bias binding.

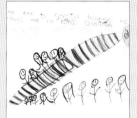

Original artwork by Emma Delery, age 5, 2007. "My Daddy" was a gift for a friend, created from a group of pictures in a booklet made by his daughter Emma Delery at school for father's day in 2007. The center picture was originally drawn in crayon and pencil. I chose to recreate it using a permanent black fine tip marker to resemble the fine pencil line and then color it with crayons. The sayings around the edge came from four different pictures and the yellow suns with orange swirls were on a number of the pages in the book; these were traced onto the fabric using permanent fabric markers.

Hanging sleeve/label on *My Daddy*. I enlarged and traced a signature from a completely different piece of artwork from the same year.

The First Christmas

**The First Christmas, 13" x 32",
2006. Original artwork by
Jenny Shirley, age 7, 1998.**
Jenny retyped an entire
Christmas book she wanted
to illustrate. After creating all
of the pictures, it seems as if
she was losing steam, as she
only ever colored the cover
and one other page. I loved the
illustrations, especially the one
of the three wise men standing
by baby Jesus. The expressions
on their faces have always
made me laugh. I decided to
recreate the cover and two of
my favorite pages in permanent
fabric marker. Jenny's color
choices on the cover were used
as the inspiration for the coloring
the other two pages. I love the
nontraditional Christmas colors
of this piece; it continues to
bring me great joy.

Far away in the East, a bright new star
appeared in the sky. Three Wise Men saw
the star and they knew that it was to tell
them that a new baby king had been born.

The First Christmas

Retold by Lynne Bradbury
Illustrated by Jenny Shirley

The three Wise Men went into the stable and
saw their baby king. They gave Him
presents of gold, frankincense and myrrh
before they left to go back to their own land.

Joseph made a bed of hay for Mary. The donkey and an ox watched over her.

A Very Happy Moment, 39" x 32", 2011. I decided that someda[y] I would enlarge my favorite page of Jenny's book and recreate it i[n] fabric and hand embroidery. Doing that would take much longer, but I believed it would be a really fun piece to work on and display! I bega[n] by enlarging my favorite page of the book to 200%. As I looked at i[t] I thought about the possibility of adding other pictures from the boo[k] to create a larger scene depicting the first Christmas.

Original artwork by Jenny Shirley, age 7, 1998. I chose the star, which had been on several pages, the ox and donkey from another page, and the sheep and angels from yet other pages. I enlarged some of the images 200%. When I enlarged the angels 200% however they were way too big; 150% proved to be just right. The sheep were already the right size.

On a hillside near Bethlehem some shepherds were watching over their sheep through the night.

Various details from A Very Happy Moment. The entire piece is made with fusible appliqué and hand embroidery. Some details are added with fabric markers. Choosing whether to border this one or not was difficult for me. I toyed with facing it, adding a multi colored chevron border, and other options before settling on framing it with a mitered border. The brown was too plain so I appliquéd holly leaves and berries in each of the corners. Using the walking foot I quilted the background with rays from the star. The rest of the quilt was free motion quilted.

The shepherds were very happy at the good news and went to Bethlehem to find the stable.

Because I often don't plan an entire quilt out before I start, I usually see something in the piece that I would change if I were to make it again. In this piece, I would change the positions of the additional drawings because the angels and the sheep are mainly white. I would reverse the ox, donkey, and sheep, so that there was some white on the left side of the quilt. The more quilts you design yourself, the more often you will think of these things in advance, but sometimes when you are on a roll and having fun, you don't notice certain details until after you are well on your way to finishing the project. Don't fret about it; these pieces are supposed to be fun. Remember, relax and let your inner child play!

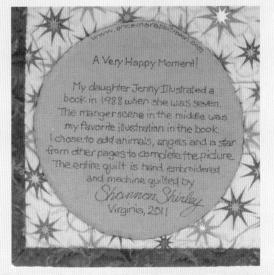

A Very Happy Moment!

My daughter Jenny illustrated a book in 1988 when she was seven. The manger scene in the middle was my favorite illustration in the book. I chose to add animals, angels and a star from other pages to complete the picture. The entire quilt is hand embroidered and machine quilted by

Shannon Shirley
Virginia, 2011

Thankful

Original artwork by Emma Shirley, age 6, 1995. This piece was done in crayon on grey construction paper. I loved all the detailed patterns that my daughter Emma had drawn in each of the feathers; the detail actually reminded me of different fabrics so that is what I chose when I decided to recreate this piece.

Detail of *Thankful.* I used fusible appliqué with hand blanket stitch on the raw edges to recreate this piece. Other embroidery and buttons were added for embellishments on the turkey.

Labels on *Thankful.*

Thankful, 39" x 45", 2011. I traced the original drawing onto tracing paper and took it to a local office supply shop, where I enlarged it to 24 inches. I took the word "thankful" from another turkey school project from that same year and enlarged it on my home printer. I decided to add two borders, but because I wanted the plaid to line up when pieced, I worked backwards by sewing the outer border first and then carefully adding the preprinted stripe that I had fussily cut into rows. Though I carefully measured, I ended up cutting the turkey background to the wrong size. Even though I had planned for the narrow green stripe to be the seam allowance, it was pressed back flat, and I blanket stitched the two pieces together. I think because I have always designed my own quilts and let them evolve as I make them, these "mistakes" do not stress me out too much; I know I can come up with a slightly different plan and sometimes it is better than the first. Detailed free motion quilting using a variety of cotton threads and clear monofilament add texture to the quilt. I used a walking foot for some of the border quilting and added a multi colored striped bias binding. I would have used the plaid fabric for the binding, but I did not have enough. For added detail, I added beads to the inner border of the quilt as the final touch. However, always remember that if a quilt is meant to be used by a child, do not add buttons and beads as they are choking hazards for small children.

Cat Nap

Pictures arranged for layout ideas for *Cat Nap*, original artwork by Emma Shirley. *Cat Nap* started out as an idea to use several pictures of cats that Emma had drawn when she was younger. Her favorite cats were orange because they matched her orange hair color. Even now as an adult, she owns an orange cat. Thirteen original drawings were incorporated into this lap quilt. Most remained their original size, but a few were enlarged.

Graph paper layout and cutting plan for *Cat Nap*. I started by arranging the pictures and then made a map on graph paper, which determined what size to cut the background pieces. I did a lot of tracing and coloring with fabric markers; however, I wasn't happy with how the blocks were looking, but I kept working on it anyway.

Cat Nap, 48" x 50", 2011. After adding homespun plaid borders with appliquéd corner blocks and free motion quilting, I was happy with the finished product; however I noticed that there was a lot of orange on the quilt except for the bottom left, so I colored one of the flowers that I had quilted in the background.

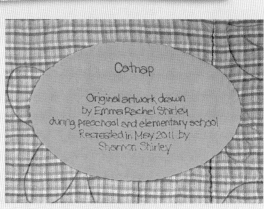

Catnap

Original artwork drawn by Emma Rachel Shirley during preschool and elementary school Recreated in May 2011 by Shannon Shirley

A Wayll of a Tail

A Wayll of a Tail, 63" x 75", 2011. On and off, for a couple of years, I have been embroidering a collection of pictures and words that my oldest daughter drew and wrote from the ages of four to ten. Some of them are from school projects or from her journal and some she created just for fun. I enlarged or reduced the originals as necessary to fit into the white squares and then traced them onto the fabric with a #2 pencil. After the embroidering was complete, I added a 1/2" green batik accent border to each square. The sashing, borders, and backing are all the same blue batik. The pictures are the main focus of the quilt, but I really like the textures in the two fabrics I chose for the quilt. The squares are free motion quilted with white cotton thread and clear monofilament. The accent borders are quilted using a walking foot and green cotton thread. The sashing and borders are quilted with a variety of multi colored cotton threads.

Details of *A Wayll of a Tail*. **Original artwork by Lauren Shirley, age 9, 1995.** Feeding rays at the Baltimore Aquarium.

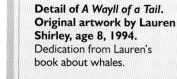

Detail of *A Wayll of a Tail*. Original artwork by Lauren Shirley, age 4, 1991. A whale from Lauren's book on animals.

Lauren has always loved marine life. At the time I started this project she had been working as an aquarist for more than four years. She worked both in and out of the water at the aquarium with many different creatures. She is now working in the oyster aquaculture field and loving it. Lauren will always have a love of water and marine life, so recreating these pictures has been a great pleasure to me. So many have memories attached to them and we will enjoy it for years to come.

Detail of *A Wayll of a Tail*. Original artwork by Lauren Shirley, age 8, 1994. Dedication from Lauren's book about whales.

Detail of *A Wayll of a Tail*. Original artwork by Lauren Shirley, 2nd grade. Cover of Lauren's book about whales.

Detail of *A Wayll of a Tail*. Lauren's favorite! Original artwork by Lauren Shirley, age 5, 1992.

January 1, 1989
There are all kinds
of fish Pretty fish, Ugley
fish, fat fish, Skiny fish, dead
fish, Ulive fish, Big fish, and
small fish.

Details of *A Wayll of a Tail*. Two pages from Lauren's journal.

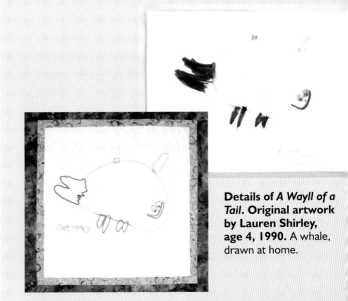

Details of *A Wayll of a Tail*. Original artwork by Lauren Shirley, age 4, 1990. A whale, drawn at home.

Details of *A Wayll of a Tail*. Original artwork by Lauren Shirley, second grade. Fish bowl, school art project.

Detail of *A Wayll of a Tail*. Original artwork by Lauren Shirley, second grade. A fish project from school.

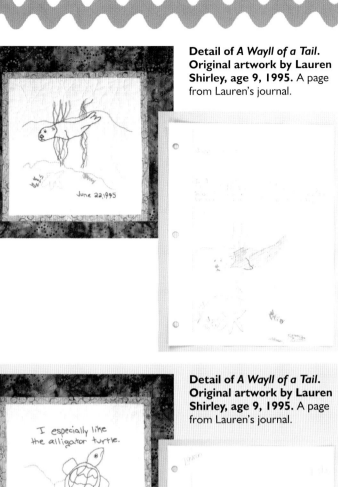

Detail of *A Wayll of a Tail*. Original artwork by Lauren Shirley, age 9, 1995. A page from Lauren's journal.

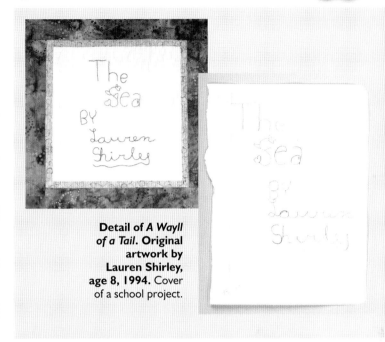

Detail of *A Wayll of a Tail*. Original artwork by Lauren Shirley, age 8, 1994. Cover of a school project.

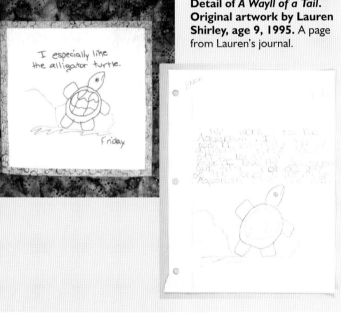

Detail of *A Wayll of a Tail*. Original artwork by Lauren Shirley, age 9, 1995. A page from Lauren's journal.

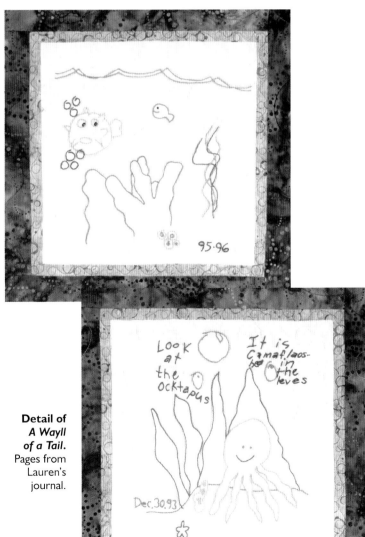

Detail of *A Wayll of a Tail*. Pages from Lauren's journal.

Detail of *A Wayll of a Tail*. Original artwork by Lauren Shirley, age 9, 1995. A page from Lauren's Journal.

Details of *A Wayll of a Tail*. **Adaptations of drawings from home.**

Original artwork by Lauren Shirley.

Chapter 6
Additional Ideas

There are so many other ideas for incorporating children's artwork into fiber art projects. Place mats, book covers, pillows, decorative towels, framed artwork, and apparel items, such as aprons, bibs, nightshirts, and children's pajamas... The possibilities are endless!

A Mom's Apron

The Kitchen Sink, **apron, 2011. Original artwork by Emma Shirley, age 7, 1995.** This picture is a still life of my old kitchen sink and the window above it. On the windowsill is my collection of vintage blue-green glass bottles, a spider plant rooting in a glass of water, and you can't miss the bottle of Joy®! Emma used markers to create the original picture. I thought about using markers as well, but instead decided to make it with fusible appliqué on an apron. Using a black fabric marker, I drew around the edge of each bottle and added details, such as the window panes, to resemble the original picture. I could have used a satin stitch around the edges, but I found it easier to draw with the marker and use a zigzag stitch. I laughed when I put the apron on for the first time and realized that the drain sat right at my belly button. From a distance I also noticed that the sink looked like an "F", so my daughter Jenny suggested I call it "'F'-rything but the Kitchen Sink!"

Tooth Fairy Pillow

MRS= 15 1st BO

DEAR TOOTHFARRE,

PLES LEV ME MY TOOTH. I WAT TO POT IT IN
MY BOOK. THAC YOU VARE VARE MACH.

LOVE
JENNY

The Toothfarre, pillow, 2011. Original artwork by Jenny Shirley, age 6, 1998. When Jenny was six and a half years old, she wrote a book about losing a tooth. She also wrote a note to the tooth fairy, using inventive spelling, asking if she could keep her tooth to put in her book. The original picture she had drawn was done in marker. I decided to make a pillow recreating the picture in fusible fabric appliqué. I added a pocket on the pillow so a child could leave their tooth and a note for the tooth fairy. I wrote the words from her book and letter on fabric which I trimmed with a pinking rotary cutter and sealed with Fray Block®. This enabled me to keep the whole story together for future enjoyment.

MY TOOTH
BY JENNY SHIRLEY

I HAD A TOOTH,
I FELLT IT AND IT WAZ LCOS.
I WIGLD IT ALL NIT,
AND I WIGLD IT All DAY.
I WIGLD IT WITH CHLSE
AND HANNAH ON THE BUS,
BUT IT DIDT FALL AWT.
ONE DAY I WAZ ETING A DORITO
AND IT FELL AWT.
MY TOOTH, I SAD.
AND THE NACST MOONI I FAWD
THREE DALLERS
WDR MY PILLOWS.
THE END

DEAR TOOTHFARRE,
PLES LEV ME MY TOOTH.
I WAT TO POT IT IN MY BOOK.
THAC YOU VARE VARE MACH.
LOVE JENNY

The text and letter Jenny wrote in inventive spelling.

Book Cover

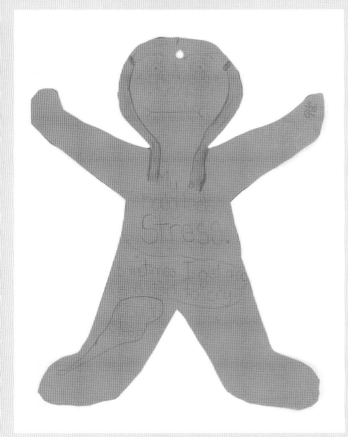

The front and back covers of *Stress* binder, 2011.

Two sides of an original artwork by Emma Shirley, done when she was in the third grade.

The front and inside cover of *Stress* binder, 2011. The original two-sided piece of artwork that inspired this project was made by Emma in the third grade. I saw this green fabric at a store. It had words printed on it having to do with relaxing and it made me think of this pink person from the original artwork. I decided to make a binder cover with it because it has a front and a back. It could just as easily be a cover for a journal, photo album, or an address book. I made tracings of the two sides, first with pencil, and then retraced them in marker. Using a window as a light box, I traced the outline of the images in reverse onto lightweight fusible and cut away the centers before fusing it to the back of the pink fabric. After cutting out the two bodies, the details were added onto the pink fabric using permanent fabric markers. I drew the diagonal quilting lines using a blue water soluble marker and sewed them using a walking foot, starting and stopping each time I came to the edge of a pink person. Quilting the background before adding the appliqué would have been much easier. It was not until after I had finished this piece and saw it in a photograph that I noticed the words on the green fabric were running in only two directions, not four as I had originally thought. This means the background fabric is upside down in my project. So… breathe, relax, slow down. These things happen to everyone.

Pillowcase

McChesney's Dragon, **pillowcase, 2011. Original artwork by Jenny Shirley, third grade.** I made this pillowcase for Jenny from a small drawing she made in the third grade while they were learning about China. The original was drawn in crayon. I love how the colors are blended. In recreating the dragon, I used crayons as well to color it in, against my better judgment. Fortunately, Jenny used this more as a decorative pillow, so we only had to occasionally hand wash it in cool water.

Afterword

Finding inspiration from children's artwork is addictive! As I have said throughout the pages of this book there are endless ways to incorporate children's artwork into a quilt or fiber art project. The level of difficulty and the time commitment are yours to choose. Mix and match techniques and finishing methods to suit your tastes. These projects make great gifts for teachers, parents, grandparents, day care providers and anyone who has a special child in their life. Chances are that child has created some artwork. I hope I have inspired you with the stories behind my quilts as well as the variety of techniques, tools and projects I have shared in the pages of this book. It is amazing what you can create when you are inspired, especially through the eyes of a child and their artwork.

Gallery

From the Classroom

I have enjoyed teaching and sharing what I have learned over the years. I love to see what my students create. Here are quilts created by some of my students.

Hope's Fox, 17" x 17", by Marianne Gravely, Lake Ridge, Virginia, 2008. Original artwork by Hope Gravely, preschool, 1999. When I signed up for Shannon's "Recreating Children's Artwork" class, I went digging in the box where I have saved my children's artwork over the years. I loved this colorful picture of a snow scene with Hope talking to a fox. She doesn't remember why she was talking to a fox, but I love the colors and the attentive pose of the fox. I used fusible appliqué for the trees, the fox, and Hope. The snowman, the birds, and Hope's signature are machine-embroidered.

Bug's Life, by Maureen Stableford, Dumfries, Virginia, 2008. Original artwork by Sean Stableford, age 5, 1998. I have my own "craft room," and when my grandson, Sean, and his older sister, Seychelle, would come over, it was always "let's make something!" We would make something together. Sean always wanted some paper and was constantly drawing, and he was very careful to get every detail. He was five when he drew "Bug's Life." Sean and Seychelle are now in college and are still very creative.

A Bear, 17" x 20", by Jane Miller, Montclair, Virginia, 2008. Original artwork by Nate Miller, age 2, 1985. When Shannon offered her class, Recreating Children's Artwork, in 2008, I knew I had to pay homage to a red-ink drawing my son had presented to me years ago. The date was December 20, 1985, and our son was around 2-1/2 years old. With the Christmas holidays and all of the excitement and to-do tasks looming, one can imagine how many loose ends there were to wrap-up! Out of the chaos, I remember my son approaching me with a piece of paper, saying "I drawed this for you, Mommy." Stopping whatever I was doing, I gazed down to Nate's angelic face and asked for his interpretation of his masterpiece. He responded "It's a Bear."

Marie's Snowman, 10" x 30", by Marianne Gravely, Lake Ridge, Virginia, 2011. Original artwork by Marie Gravely, first grade, 1998. I loved this robust snowman, surrounded by snowflakes, that my daughter Marie drew when she was in first grade. I hand appliquéd the snowman and his broom, and used an assortment of buttons for the snowflakes and the decorations on the snowman. Since the buttons are all different, they mimic the playfulness of her original drawing.

The Underwater World, 34" x 35", by Vania Root, Woodbridge, Virginia, 2011. Original artwork by Matthew Root, second grade 2005-06. When I took Shannon's class, "Recreating Children's Artwork," I decided to recreate a picture my son Matthew drew when he was in second grade. As you can see, the original was drawn in pencil, which left all of the colors options up to me. I used fusible appliqué for most of the picture, but to me the stick figures called for a satin stitch. Everything that I quilted in color was in the original drawing; the textures and details that I quilted in monofilament were my artistic additions.

Kathleen's Art Work, 31" x 26", by Ginny Rippe, Manassas, Virginia, 2011. Original artwork by Kathleen Rippe, age 9, 1994. My daughter Kathleen used watercolors for this painting. She was nine years old and in the fourth grade. The water scene was inspired by the *Little Mermaid*, a popular movie at the time. I used a variety of batik fabrics to interpret the painting into a quilt and free motion quilted it with cotton threads. If you look closely in the bottom border, I quilted my daughter's name, grade, age, and the year she created the original art. I began the quilt in Shannon Shirley's "Recreating Children's Artwork" class in June 2011 and completed it in October 2011.

From the Author

Appendix

Product List

Blue water soluble marker by Clover and Wrights
www.createforless.com
www.joann.com

Crayola crayons and pencils
www.Crayola.com

Detail craft knife by Fiskars
www.Fiskars.com

Fabric Mate Markers by Yasutomo
www.Yasutomo.com

Fabrico Markers by Tsukineko
www.Tsukineko.com

Flat Sash Rods by Kirsch®
www.kirsch.com

Fray Block by June Tailor
www.JuneTailor.com

Heat n Bond Lite by Therm O Web
www.thermowebonline.com

Inktense water soluble ink pencils by Derwent
www.pencils.co.uk

Jacquard Paints
www.jacquardproducts.com

Lightweight fusible stabilizer by Pellon
www.shoppellon.com

Marvy Markers by Uchida
www.Marvy.com

Micron Pen – by Sakura of America
www.sakuraofamerica.com

Monofilament by Sulky
www.Sulky.com

Non-Stick Pressing Sheet by June Tailor
www.JuneTailor.com

Peltex 72 by Pellon
www.shoppellon.com

Pinking rotary cutter by Olfa Products
www.Olfa.com

Prang crayons
www.Prang.com

Prismacolor pencils by Sanford
www.Prismacolor.com

Quilter's Assistant Proportional Scale by Golden
   Threads
www.GoldenThreads.com

Saral wax free transfer paper by Saral Paper
   Company
www.SaralPaper.com

Sequin Pins (half inch) by Dritz
www.dritz.com

So Soft fabric paint by Tulip
www.duncancrafts.com

Tracer projector and enlarger by Artograph
www.Artograph.com

Glossary

Accent Border: A narrow inner border often using a contrasting color fabric.

Bias Binding: Binding made from strips that are cut at a 45-degree angle to the grain of the fabric. You must use this if there are any curves on your border as it has more give than straight binding.

Blind Hem Stitch: Many machines offer this as a hemming stitch, but it can be adjusted very narrow and can be used to machine applique shapes in place giving the appearance of very tiny hand stitching.

Blanket Stitch: Hand embroidery stitch that can be used to finish the raw edge of fusible applique. Many machines offer this as a decorative stitch as well.

Couching: A technique where yarn, string, or ribbon are laid onto a fabric and held in place with stitches done over the top by machine or hand.

Edge Stitch: A row of stitching placed very close to the edge of a quilt, usually 14" or less.

Escape Hatch Method: This is when you use two pieces of fabric for the back, seam them together leaving the center of the seam open, place the back face down on the front, and sew all the way around the edge. Then turn the project right side out through the opening you left in the seam.

Facing: A clean edge alternative to a traditional binding, added after the quilting is done. A fabric frame is added to the front of the quilt and then turned to the back and stitched in place by hand.

Free Motion Quilting: Drop the feed dogs on a sewing machine and stitch in any direction you choose. You are the feed dog and can freely move around the quilt.

French knots: Hand embroidery stitch that resembles a knot. Often it is used for eyes, seeds or other small dots.

Fussy cut: When cutting a novelty print fabric, you carefully cut particular designs one at a time.

Heat set: Many products need to be heat set with a hot dry iron. Sometimes this process makes the product permanent and other times it removes excess color from the project.

Knife Edge: The quilt top and the quilt back meet evenly at the edge of the quilt.

Ladder stitch: A hand stitch that when tightened the stitches are virtually invisible.

Mitered (border/facing): Four pieces of fabric that are pieced at a 45 degree angle at the corners, like a frame.

Outline Stitch: Hand embroidery stitch used to create a line whether straight or curvy. Stitching pictures is very easy using this stitch.

Sashing: Fabric pieces that go between blocks in a quilt top, can be simple or complex.

Sleeve: A tube of fabric that you attach to the top back of a quilt to allow it to be hung.

Straight of grain/cross grain: Straight of grain follows the warp thread and is parallel to the selvage, it has very little give. The cross grain follows the weft thread and has slightly more give.

Thread Sketching: Drop the feed dogs and draw with your sewing machine. Very similar to free motion quilting but using smaller stitches and contrasting thread.

Walking Foot: A specialty foot made for most sewing machine that helps handle the bulky layers of a quilt. Very useful when machine quilting straight lines.